The Fabian Society

The Fabian Society is Britain's leading left of centre think tank and political society, committed to creating the political ideas and policy debates which can shape the future of progressive politics.

With over 300 Fabian MPs, MEPs, Peers, MSPs and AMs, the Society plays an unparalleled role in linking the ability to influence policy debates at the highest level with vigorous grassroots debate among our growing membership of over 7000 people, 70 local branches meeting regularly throughout Britain and a vibrant Young Fabian section organising its own activities. Fabian publications, events and ideas therefore reach and influence a wider audience than those of any comparable think tank. The Society is unique among think tanks in being a thriving, democratically-constituted membership organisation, affiliated to the Labour Party but organisationally and editorially independent.

For over 120 years Fabians have been central to every important renewal and revision of left of centre thinking. The Fabian commitment to open and participatory debate is as important today as ever before as we explore the ideas, politics and policies which will define the next generation of progressive politics in Britain, Europe and around the world. Find out more at **www.fabians.org.uk**

Fabian Society
11 Dartmouth Street
London SW1H 9BN
www.fabians.org.uk

Fabian ideas
Editorial Director: Tom Hampson

First published 2006

ISBN 0 7163 0619 0

British Library Cataloguing in Publication data.
A catalogue record for this book is available from the British Library.

Printed and bound by Bell & Bain, Glasgow

2025

What next for the
Make Poverty History generation?

Introduction by Hilary Benn

Tom Hampson, Robert Cooper,
Clare Short, Vandana Shiva and
Michelle Harrison

FABIAN SOCIETY

Acknowledgments

The editor would like to thank Debbie Porter at DFID, Marion Colverd at TUFM, David Ellis at the Fabian Society, and Jason Rochin.

The trends analysis and scenario development on which Michelle Harrison's article is based was undertaken by a team of people from Henley Centre Headlight Vision: Gemma Stevenson, Rachel Goodacre, Rachel Kelnar, Billie Moseley and Jennifer Kivett.

We would especially like to thank TUFM for their generous support.

Contents

About the authors

Robert Cooper is Director General for External and Politico-Military Affairs at the General Secretariat of the Council of the European Union. He was brought up in Britain and Kenya, returning from Nairobi to the UK to attend Oxford University (Worcester College, PPE) in 1966. He spent a year at the University of Pennsylvania in Philadelphia joining the Diplomatic Service in 1970.

He has served in New York, Tokyo, Brussels and Bonn. His Foreign Office career was divided broadly between Asia and Europe. From 1989 to 1993 he was Head of the Policy Planning Staff. Later in the 1990s he was Director for Asia and was then Deputy Secretary for Defence and Overseas Affairs in the Cabinet Office. Before moving to Brussels in 2002 he was Special Representative for the British Government on Afghanistan. He has published a number of essays and articles on international affairs and, most recently, a book of essays: 'The Breaking of Nations', Atlantic Press 2003.

Tom Hampson is Editorial Director of the Fabian Society where he commissions and edits all Fabian publications and is Editor of the *The Fabian Review*. Tom joined the Fabians in January 2006 and continues to run his own media and public affairs consultancy The Press Company, specialising in social issues clients.

He was previously Media Communication Manager for Sarah Brown at Hobsbawm Macaulay and served as Communications Manager at the think tank Demos from 1997 to 2000. Tom has recently written on equality and human rights, education policy, disability, international development, and the renewal of the British left.

Dr Michelle Harrison leads the Public Sector consultancy practice at Henley Centre Headlight Vision. She is the author of 'King Sugar: Jamaica, the Caribbean and the international sugar trade', (Latin American Bureau 2001) which explores the relationship between trade, transnational corporations and development.

Dr Vandana Shiva trained as a physicist – her PhD is on quantum theory. In 1982, she founded an independent institute, the Research Foundation for Science, Technology and Ecology in Dehra Dun dedicated to high quality and independent research to address the most significant ecological and social issues of our times, in close partnership with local communities and social movements.

In 1991, she founded Navdanya, a national movement to protect the diversity and integrity of living resources, especially native seed, the promotion of organic farming and fair trade. Navdanya works with local communities and organisations serving more than two million men and women farmers.

Dr Shiva is based in New Delhi and has been a visiting professor and lectured at the University of Oslo in Norway, Schumacher College in the UK, Mount Holyoke College in the US, York University and the University of Victoria in Canada, the University of Lulea in Sweden, and the Université Libre de Bruxelles in Belgium.

Time magazine identified Dr Shiva as an environmental 'hero' in 2003 and *Asia Week* has called her one of the five most powerful communicators of Asia.

Rt Hon Clare Short MP was Secretary of State for International Development from 1997 to May 2003. DFID was a new ministry created after the 1997 general election to promote policies for sustainable development and the elimination of poverty and it manages Britain's programme of assistance to developing countries.

She entered the House of Commons in 1983 as MP for Birmingham Ladywood where she was born and had grown up. From 1996 until the 1997 general election she was the Opposition spokesperson on overseas development. She was Shadow Minister for Women from 1993 to 1995 and Shadow Secretary of State for Transport from 1995 to 1996. She has also been Opposition spokesperson on environment protection, social security and employment. Clare Short's book 'An Honourable Deception? New Labour, Iraq, and the Misuse of Power' was published in 2004 by Free Press.

Introduction

Hilary Benn

The first generation of Fabians got straight to the point, calling their inaugural pamphlet in 1884 'Why are the Many Poor?' It is a question we still have to ask today. While there are a thousand billionaires around the world, over a billion people live in extreme poverty. Why are the many *still* poor? And what can we do about it?

It is almost sixty years since the Universal Declaration of Human rights proclaimed every human being's right to education, to health and social security, and to an adequate standard of living.

The Make Poverty History coalition was born of that same progressive tradition that helped change so many lives in Britain. As developing countries progress they face the same questions as Britain has over the last century. How can they meet their responsibility to provide social security and basic services for all their citizens? The challenge now – for all of us – is to support countries to change things for the better for poor people across the world.

In a world of 24-hour news coverage, we see what is happening across the world and we have a choice, as we had a choice in Britain. We can choose to turn our backs and do nothing, or we can decide to help. That's what made a difference in 2005. The power of ordinary people calling not for charity but for justice, itself a recognition of our increasingly interdependent world. Many problems – like conflicts, pollution and diseases such as HIV and AIDS – are caused or made worse by poverty. What happens on the other side of the world affects us all. So it is not only our moral responsibility to act, it is also in our interest to do so.

Here we are at the beginning of the 21st century and yet we know that in the developing world, pregnancy and childbirth claim the life of a woman every minute – women who die alone and afraid on the floor of a darkened hut with no midwife or doctor to help.

6,000 children will die today from a lack of clean water to drink. Each year – every year – malaria kills one million people, tuberculosis kills two million people, AIDS kills three million people. Every death is a human life extinguished and an individual's potential unfulfilled.

Of the children who do live beyond the age of five, over 100 million of them are not where they should be: in school. They can't go to school because it costs too much, or because they have to work, or because they are orphans. For those who do survive to adulthood, many become destitute because of the cost of medical care. They have to sell what little they have – their chickens or goats – to pay for medicines, leaving them unable to earn a living. Or they can't afford medicine at all. And for those who finally make to it to old age there are no pensions. Those with no family to support them have to beg to live.

And all of this is happening in a developing world that is changing at a bewildering speed. Within three decades the urban populations of Africa, Asia and Latin America will double to nearly 4 billion human beings. By 2020 the majority of Asian men and women will be living in towns and cities. By 2035 the same will be true of most Africans.

The story to come over the next decades is one that finds echoes in our own past. From the industrial revolution and those great social reformers who went to the mills and the factories, and the villages and the slums, and reported back on conditions and helped change things for the better. Through the School Meals Act of 1906, which made sure that children could study rather than being too hungry to concentrate. The 1911 National Insurance Act putting in place the beginnings of an old age pension. The Beveridge report in 1942 which set out to slay the

'Five Giants" – poverty, disease, squalor, ignorance and idleness – that held people back. Beveridge could have been talking about the lives of poor people in the developing world, because this is the same challenge we face today but on a global scale. The Make Poverty History campaign is the global equivalent of the social reformers of the 19th century.

I welcome this book because it focuses on the future and I believe passionately that is what we need to do. As we do so we should draw comfort and encouragement from what we achieved in 2005. Did we make poverty history? No. Did we make progress? Yes. The UK, as President of the G8, pushed for change in the run up to Gleneagles and at the summit itself. And we got agreement from the world's richest countries to: increase aid by $50 billion a year by 2010 with half of that money earmarked for Africa; write off the debts of the world's 19 poorest countries; launch an international facility for immunisation that aims to vaccinate and save the lives of five million children over the next decade; and set the goal of trying to get AIDS treatment for everyone in the developing world who needs it by 2010.

But it is what we do now and in the years ahead that will make the difference. That's partly about keeping the promises we made at Gleneagles – things we can do on aid, trade and debt relief. But it's also about Africa and other developing countries taking the decisions they need to.

The UK has a rising aid budget and we're using it to help countries to train the teachers and doctors, build the schools, buy the drugs, provide the clean water and help the farmers with seeds or irrigation or electricity. But developing countries also need to be able to build their economies with investment, jobs and income – to have the chance to earn their way out of poverty.

And for all of this to happen developing countries need good governance. We need to support them to do the things that we look to our government to do: to uphold the law; to decide where to spend public money; to support the most vulnerable in society; and, above all, to answer to the people of the country. It's about making politics work to change things for the better, in the best Fabian tradition.

Progressive politics has changed the face of Britain. It is now up to all of us to make this change global. We know the challenge we face and what needs to be done. So let's just get on with it.

The Rt Hon Hilary Benn MP
Secretary of State
International Development
July 2006

1 | Twelve months on

Tom Hampson

Dreams and disappointment have long been the emotional food and drink of the British left. As British poverty campaigners – and Irish rock stars – led us by the wrist-banded arms to gorge ourselves on hope this time last year, so we are now in danger of becoming positively drunk with disappointment and cynicism on the anniversary of Live 8 and Gleneagles.

And it's not just the left – or those in 'progressive' politics as we now call ourselves. Just as it was commonplace last summer to comment on the demographic breadth of those groups that joined the anti-poverty cause (never, it would seem, had so many mothers with pushchairs, suited businessmen, Rastafarian children and their grandmothers been seen together in one place) so it is now hard to find many people – inside or outside politics – who claim that the global poverty campaign of 2005 was anything other than a wash out. It was always a patronising misreading of the public mood to call Live 8 'just a pop concert' – people really believed in it and had made considered judgments about what it could achieve. Such public disillusionment now could put the progress made last year at risk.

National narratives are important in times of collective action and as soon as Paul McCartney left the Live 8 stage the narrative demanded we felt let down and deflated. The London bombings – often linked in our minds with the Olympics, but actually designed to wreck the opening day of Gleneagles – helped us see our collective hubris for what it really was.

And the truth is it was hard for most of us to know who to believe anyway. What really was achieved? Some of the more bolshie NGOs complained of a lack of much more substantial commitments on aid – let alone the increase to 0.7 percent of national income they had called for. This troubled many, who were left with the suspicion that western powers were using debt relief as a way of strong-arming African states into the harsh blast of free market economics.

Bono came away from Gleneagles with his characteristic air of mock-humility but also a certain ebullience: "If an Irish rock star can quote Winston Churchill, I wouldn't say this is the end of extreme poverty, but it is the beginning of the end." Kumi Naidoo, Chair of the Global Call for Action Against Poverty, summed up the feelings of many NGOs, though, when he said that "the people have roared but the G8 has whispered".

Anyhow, by now the dull thuds of rucksack bombs under London had drawn Blair back to the capital and drawn our collective gaze inwards and downwards. The news agenda moved on so quickly it felt like an early end to Summer.

With the benefit of twelve months' hindsight, though, Hilary Benn's list of the achievements of 2005 should give us some pause:

> Agreement from the world's richest countries to increase aid by $50 billion a year by 2010 with half of that money earmarked for Africa; agreement to write off the debts of the world's 19 poorest countries; we launched an international facility for immunisation that aims to vaccinate and save the lives of five million children over the next decade; we set the goal of trying to get AIDS treatment for everyone in the developing world who needs this by 2010.

In fact, the lesson of 2005 must be that the case for progressive action *can* be argued and that real change *can* result. The danger is in the very doubt itself. Fashionable, weary cynicism can very easily turn to the reactionary. The calculation made by Oxfam, Save the Children and the other members of the coalition in coming together, campaigning, educating, and raising hopes in the way they did was a correct one. Make Poverty History did raise the bar and made real headway and we underestimate the success of the project at our peril. It revealed that – when given the power to influence debates on a global scale – the British public have become very progressive in their instincts.

Indeed, Make Poverty History saw the coming of age of the British protest movement. This was the first time a protest movement had been truly mainstream. You can draw a straight, upward line that begins with the small groups of people who marched on Aldermaston in 1958, passes through Greenham, Greenpeace, and Amnesty, past Live Aid in 1985 and the increasingly mainstream loyalty to brands like Oxfam and

Twenty years on from Live8, 40 years on from Live Aid, will Britain be in a position to lead global change in 2025? Will we still care? Well, it depends who we have become.

concepts of fair trade goods, past Jubilee 2000, through the (still minority) anti-war movements and marches in 2001, and towards Live 8 in 2005. And whereas Live Aid in 1985 had operated in a kind of implicit opposition to Margaret Thatcher (whose misjudgment of the public mood extended to clawing back all the VAT from the Band Aid singles and publicly arguing with Geldof) the Labour government, and Gordon Brown in particular, were wholeheartedly onside in 2005.

The public is increasingly aware that alongside the globalisation of markets and information, power has shifted beyond the nation state. We are also aware that the international bodies that could democratise that power now seem poorly suited to the task. The global Make Poverty History coalition in all its various guises – it was called 'ONE' in the United States, for example, and spanned more than 40 countries around the world – succeeded briefly in providing a body that functioned in that international space, appeared intelligently aware of its mandate and the limits of that mandate. It was – to use the Prime Minister's phrase – fit for purpose. As multinational. progressive, democratic and interventionist bodies go, it worked very well.

The momentum wasn't sustained after July. But much of the potential will and passion is still there. The question that now faces us is how to learn from and emulate it.

This is why public engagement in our development and foreign policies is crucial. In a democracy, public support has always been necessary when entering into conflicts. Development is no different. If we are to meet the Millennium Development Goals of halving extreme poverty and halting HIV/Aids by 2015 and if we are to move towards the role we want Britain to have in the world of 2025 we will need to see the democratisation of our foreign policy. The British public have shown both the capacity and the desire to engage in shaping foreign policy and Make Poverty History showed that positive and progressive public debate can be won.

The task before us now is to find ways to continue the engagement, to look honestly at British attitudes to the rest of the world, to global aid and to our responsibilities to other countries, to describe the Britain we want to see over the coming decades and to predict the drivers that could stop us getting there.

Twenty years on from Live 8, 40 years on from Live Aid, will Britain be in a position to lead global change in 2025? Will the British public still care? Well, it depends who we have become. It is in realistically describing the Britain we want that the Henley Centre's scenarios are so useful. Their team worked to design 60 drivers, ranging from the nature of our ageing population, the urbanisation of culture, and perceptions of climate change, to the rise of single-issue politics and extremism. From the rise of China and India, the time deficit, information overload, gender inequality, and water scarcity to growing NGO activity and the perception of corruption in developing countries.

Using these drivers they have mapped out the likely territory of our future. In one of their four scenarios, Henley describes a Britain where consumers are very aware of the effect their actions have on their community and the rest of the world. Henley – with more than a hint of irony – calls this 2025 scenario 'The 'Good' Life':

> The majority of households now have direct debits set up to charities. These days, however, those who donate to international development charities make a direct debit into the bank account of the female head of household of the family that they sponsor. Under this scenario the NGOs compete for the role of 'best international connector'. They also have developed a strong brand around long haul travel advice: helping travellers do 'the maximum overland and the minimum over cloud' ... Interest in debt, trade and aid issues remains strong but it is climate change that has risen to the top of the political agenda.

This is a vision of a rather different Britain to the one we live in now. But compare it to another 2025 scenario, named 'Choice Unlimited' by Henley:

> Oxfam and Greenpeace compete to be known for giving the best parties and, in order to maintain crowd numbers at campaigning rallies, now market them as festivals... National government is continuing to focus on economic growth and less than ten percent of people vote in the local authority elections. Trade and aid issues remain on the political agenda thanks to continued NGO lobbying. But consumer pressure is weak – even single issue campaigns are failing to achieve genuine political momentum.

None of these scenarios is designed to be good or bad *per se*. And, as Michelle Harrison says, "These scenarios are rehearsals. We know that the future could dish up any mix of these potential extremes."

What they do, though, is define a clear – and highly political – dividing line. Those of us on the centre-left *should* be doing all we can to move us towards 'The 'Good' Life'. We *don't* believe that consumerism (or, for that matter, the Puritanism or insolationism of the other Henley scenarios) holds the answers or should define our global identity. This is not something even the wettest Tory could agree with. We must be realistic about where society is and where it could go, but that doesn't mean we can't campaign for the vision of the Britain we want.

However, we will have to prepare to deal with some obstacles on the way. Henley data shows that the number of people saying that the government should spend more money on the poor has consistently fallen every year since 1989. They also show that in 2005 – for the first time since 1994 – there were more people in the UK who thought quality of life was best improved by looking after themselves rather than their communities. Perhaps Live 8 and Make Poverty History captured an aspect of our 'better selves' – a glimpse of the society we would really like to be.

We must recognise that one of the most damaging obstacles to the democratisation of our foreign policy has been Iraq. Just as Tony Blair called Africa 'the stain on the conscience of humanity' so Iraq has now become the stain on the conscience of the left. The war and the perception that Labour's second term was dominated by an adherence to the White House's view of the middle east has coloured everything. Clare Short must be right to argue that unless the West succeeds in fostering a peace process that promotes justice in the middle east, there will be no basis on which to build global sustainable development and a more equitable balance of power and wealth.

However, Short is just as persuasive when she observes that the enormity of the dangers we face "are more seriously understood by people in the UK and elsewhere than by the global elite". Finding ways to make clear links between people and policy will provide some of the keys. An international development force – a kind of territorial army of police, administrators, engineers and lawyers – as Robert Cooper envisages, could go some way to make that link.

It is also about using our creativity and skills. Amitai Etzioni has written of the two types of globalisation. In addition to the opening up of global trade, of massive multinationals, and the globalisation of the free market there is also the unstoppable and largely benign global technological and communications revolution. Mobile communications, mass media and the Internet are all essentially emancipatory and democratic developments and British foreign policy can learn the lessons from Make Poverty History in how to use them to progressive ends. Finding our role in the world is not only part of a continual process of rediscovering who we are, but of understanding our power to manage and catalyse change.

In some ways, the dreams and disappointment of the last year are simply the latest chapter in the British post-war story of coming to terms with our loss of empire. In Labour's first two terms, the calculation has been that an edgy balancing act which triangulated our relationship with Europe and America was the answer. It is hard to argue that this strategy has served the Blair administration well in the eyes of the world. Cooper makes the point that it will not be good enough for the British just to mobilise themselves – we must mobilise other countries too. Our postcolonial doubts about Britain's role in the world aren't held only by the British. Vandana Shiva eloquently paints a picture of Britain that much of the world still holds. A selfish, greedy, elderly giant, emasculated and self-centred. This is not a view of Britain that we can be comfortable with.

As the role of China and India on the world stage increases over the next two decades, telling a progressive story about our role will need to be a central part of what an incoming Brown administration does. As the Labour Party goes through a process of renewal, thinking about our global reputation will be crucial. "Inch by inch, he is dragging his party into the warm sunshine of credibility" is how a rather optimistic *Daily Telegraph* leader recently described David Cameron's process of renewing the Conservative Party. The far greater task Gordon Brown will have in restoring Britain's global reputation will be no less slow and painful.

We need to ask ourselves why it was the British (or, perhaps more accurately Scots and Dubliners based in London) who, of all the Western peoples, felt the moral certainty last year to intervene and proselytise. We need to recognise that our role must draw on the benefits of our history of empire and we need to cast Britain in an enabling, educated and campaigning role. That role must be based in a belief in democracy and good governance but, just as strongly, in a progressive passion for equality, justice and the desire to use globalisation as a force for good. We need to listen to the anger of those like Shiva but also recognise we have wisdom in our experience, and the responsibility that comes with that. We must also recognise – as apparently even Oliver Letwin does now – that eradicating UK child poverty must happen within this generation. If we can't make poverty history at home, how can we hope to do so elsewhere?

Live Aid is invariably now written about as if it came out of a more innocent time, when we were young and green. Actually, in 1985 we doing far more than just rattling tins and asking for money. Live Aid saw an emerging moral certainty from the progressive left, born of the activism of the 1970s and early 1980s and bravely struggling out from under the dead weight of Nigel Lawson and Thatcherism. It infected the whole country for that summer. It spread from Wembley to the United States and around the world. Even forty years on, it should be our inspiration.

2 | First we must change ourselves

Clare Short MP

There are two different futures on offer. In the first, we create a just settlement in the Middle East and thus reduce and contain the threat from Al Qaeda, strengthen international law and the multilateral institutions that are focused on the reduction of poverty, share the planet's natural resources more fairly and sustainably and contain the risk of global warming. This will require a more equitable world order and a different and less materialistic way of life in which we consume less fossil fuel.

The alternative future is the one we are currently heading towards. Continuing to follow the road we are now on will intensify the suffering of the Palestinian people and lead us further into the quagmire in Iraq, thereby increasing the threat from Al Qaeda, weakening international law and the authority of the United Nations, and intensifying the competition for oil and other natural resources. As the world's population moves from six billion to nine billion over the coming decades, following our current strategy will also mean we fail to address the growth in poverty concentrated in the mega-cities of the developing world, fail to contain nuclear proliferation, and fail to address global warming and the strain on our environmental resources. This will increase poverty, disorder, conflict and the frequency of environmental crises.

These dangers are so great that serious scholars argue that if we do not make major changes in the way we live over the next 30 years, we could well be advancing towards the end of human civilisation on the planet within the next two centuries.

The enormity of the dangers we face – which I believe are more seriously understood by citizens in the UK and elsewhere than by the global elite – can cause people to give up in despair or to laugh off the dangers in the way the Bush administration does.

At a recent meeting of the All Party Group on Climate Change, the head of the UK Meteorological Office said that over the next 30 years the turbulence, drought, flooding and instability resulting from the growth of carbon dioxide emissions since the Industrial Revolution could not be halted. He stressed that a failure to take action within this period would lead to catastrophic events by 2100.

These are short time scales. There is much to be done and much that can be done. However, I am afraid that the media-driven politics with which we are now living mean that although leaders are picking up from focus groups the public's concern about poverty and global warming they are merely issuing warm words and not taking serious action to deal with the growing threat. Thus David Cameron promises that his blue will be tinged with green but believes in Thatcherite reform of the public services and a pro-American foreign policy. And Tony Blair promised that the UK Presidency of the G8 would focus on poverty in Africa and global warming but – despite huge levels of public support – little was achieved. The meeting was very successful spin, but in practice little was delivered to Africa and President Bush's intransigence ensured that there was no progress on climate change.

I do not believe it is possible for the UK to play a leading role in making poverty history unless it commits to policies that will reduce inequality at home. Narrowing the inequality gap should ensure that public opinion will support work to reduce poverty across the world and to build a less materialistic and competitive way of life.

Richard Wilkinson has made a study of comparable measures of the scale of inequality in different societies that demonstrates why –

despite their extraordinary material success – modern societies are social failures:

> In societies where income differences between rich and poor are smaller, the statistics show not only that community life is stronger and people are much more likely to trust each other, but also there is less violence – including substantially lower homicide rates – health is better and life expectancy several years longer, prison populations are smaller, birth rates among teenagers are lower, levels of educational attainment among school children tend to be higher, and there is more social mobility. In all cases, where income differences are narrower, outcomes are better.
>
> That's a lot to lay at the door of inequality, but all these relationships are statistically highly significant and cannot be dismissed as chance findings.[1]

It is notable that the countries that are the least unequal – the Scandinavian countries – also stand for highly progressive policies on the international stage. They provide high levels of aid, are very strong supporters of the UN, disarmament, and non-proliferation treaties. Their politics are deeply social democrat.

In my view, the tragically missed opportunity since 1997 is that just as the people of the UK were becoming much more supportive of social democratic ideas, New Labour moved away from them. The models for New Labour came from the United States – particularly from the New Democrats – which was where ideas like tax credits and Sure Start were taken from. But the Scandinavian model is one of highly efficient modern economies with high quality public services, much less inequality and a much better quality of life.

My conclusion is that the Labour government needs to change its analysis and the model of the good society to which it is working and to implement different policies at home if it is to win public support for the policies necessary to make poverty history.

I do not believe that it is possible to mobilise the influence of the UK for greater international justice, poverty reduction and sustainability on the international stage unless we stand by these values in all aspects of our foreign policy and in the way we organise our own society. There is no doubt that the occupation of Iraq, failure to support a just peace for the Palestinians or to halt the displacement and suffering of the people of Darfur and Congo are all undermining International Law, respect for human rights and the authority of the UN. The same can be said of the existence of Guantanamo Bay, the Abu Ghraib prison and extraordinary rendition. On all of these issues the UK has become the automatic ally of the United States.

In addition, the Bush administration's failure to ratify the Kyoto treaty or support the International Criminal Court is a major setback for multilateralism. But, despite paying lip service to these values, the UK continues its intimate and almost unconditional support for an extreme and unwise US administration. This makes it impossible for the European Union to stand together behind a better approach to global problems.

> **If we sought to combine with others to build a more just and equitable world order, the potential is enormous.**
> **Instead, Prime Ministers focus on 'the special relationship'.**

I am very sad to say that Labour's commitment to international development – which has been central to the party since the days of Harold Wilson – no longer underpins our foreign policy and is now little more than a piece of triangulation.

The UK is now the fifth or sixth largest economy in the world and as China and India grow our clout in international affairs will continue to diminish. But we still have potential to be an influence for good on the world stage. We have seats on the UN Security Council, International Monetary Fund, and World Bank boards. We have membership of the UN, the Commonwealth and the EU. If we sought to combine with others to build a more just and equitable world order, the potential would be enormous. But instead, every post war Prime Minister apart from Edward Heath has made the 'special relationship' the centrepiece of our foreign policy.

The UK faces a major choice. If we really wish to help to make poverty history and make the world safer and more sustainable, we need to commit to social democratic values and dedicate ourselves to a reduction in inequality at home. We also need a foreign policy designed to encourage a more equitable and sustainable world order. In 1997 I hoped that this was our intention but we have ended up on the wrong road.

There needs to be an intense debate uniting all progressive forces on what kind of country we want to be. We cannot play a leading role in making poverty history *and* continue to act as America's poodle. We need to choose.

References

1   Wilkinson, R. 'The Impact of Inequality: the empirical evidence', *Renewal* vol 14, no 1, 2006.

3 | What the British must do

Robert Cooper

C an the British – just one percent of the world's population – really make a difference? Yes we can, but not in isolation and only if we are organised and have a common purpose. Only if we listen, think, communicate and act with others.

We think that something must be done about the great global issues: environment and development. And we *have* done something. Yes, we have attended rock concerts and we have gone on demonstrations but, more importantly, we have got the message across to governments that they cannot win votes without putting development aid and the environment into their programmes. And if they cut aid or forget the environment they will lose electoral support. That presents us with a big opportunity.

We do not need more rock concerts. There is nothing wrong with them, but progress comes through persistence. We need to hold governments accountable to the very considerable promises they have made. We should seek regular progress reports on the commitment to increase aid: letters to MPs, questions in the House of Commons, questions at election meetings, questions on television. If we are going to ask the right questions then we need to be more demanding and more knowledgeable – and more rigorous too.

The fact is that all of the magic solutions proposed by development theorists over the last fifty years have been wrong. Citizens need to ask themselves more practical questions. Does geography as taught in schools help us understand the problems of development? Should we take anthropology more seriously to understand that other societies may have different values to our own? We should recognise our own past mistakes – including support for many rulers who were a disaster for their people. We might ask ourselves too whether there are still some unacceptable cases of double standards (while bearing in mind that life is full of dilemmas and compromises). But, for a beginning, perhaps we could be a little more ready to listen and a little less quick to classify. Especially where the classification (communist, fascist, terrorist, Islamist) is one that precludes communication.

In everything there is a role for the private sector, a role for the NGOs and a role for government. These are best not confused. The job of companies is to be responsible to the law and to their share-holders. If there is profit in doing good that is fine; if there is profit in doing bad, then the government should change the laws or the taxes. Getting the government to do this is the job of NGOs. They need to be careful not to be caught up too much in the business of making money (best left to businesses) or winning popularity (best left to the political parties). In fact if an NGO is not unpopular some-where with somebody then it is probably doing a bad job. And the job of government is to set the framework of law nationally and to negotiate the framework of co-operation – or law if you can get it – internationally. We have some stunning examples of how this can work. The best is the abolition of the slave trade. The NGO campaign at home made this the government's principal's objective from the Congress of Vienna through most of the 19th century. The campaign against landmines over the last decade has similarly changed a small piece of history.

We need to change behaviour and the most effective way to do that is through the market and the tax system. For example, something that could make a huge difference would be if Western governments put a floor under the price of oil. If we do that, industry would have a long term planning horizon and alternative energy producers will have some certainty of a return on investment. The floor price should not be static but should increase every year by a couple of percentage points above the rate of inflation.

We need to move from 'something must be done' to 'we must do something'. Maybe even one day to 'I must do something'. But do what? We should think about development not just in economic terms. Development is development of the state. It is only incidentally about economic growth. Essentially, it is about security, justice and individual freedom. If you put these together with a small amount of capital in due course you will have prosperity. The idea that giving people money makes them developed, or even rich, is a fallacy. So is giving them power stations, dams, roads, schools, hospitals. All of these can be useful but they do not, on their own, bring development. That has to come from within. 'Develop' is not a transitive verb. We cannot develop a people: they develop themselves.

> **Development is development of the state. It is only incidentally about economic growth. Essentially, it is about security, justice and individual freedom.**

Sometimes we can help provide a breathing space so they can sort out the basics of development – which are all political. The breathing space may be about preventing people from starving or it may be about providing security. The two are often brought together under the heading of human security. There is no development without security – I know somebody who helped build the same road three times in one African country. In between the different armies passed up and down the road and the jungle broke it up. (The country is astonishingly fertile.)

We should think more radically about human security and prepare for it. The questions we should ask should not be directed just at development ministries but at defence ministries too. Are our armed

forces right for the jobs they really have to do – more often consoli
dating a peace than fighting a war? Do we have enough armed forces?
Or should we think in more radical terms of a force for human security which can include police, administrators, engineers, lawyers.
Perhaps we need a kind of territorial army of such people, able to
work closely with the military but not part of it, who can be mobilised
at short notice in a crisis. If we really want to help development we
have to be professional and serious about it, the way that the military
have always been about defence. Perhaps indeed we need to rethink
the whole idea of defence. Our security in the future may depend as
much on sustainable politics – which means sustainable development
– as it once did on our borders.

But it is no good just mobilising ourselves. We need to mobilise the
world. What one percent of the world does will be lost if 20 percent
(China, in terms of population) or 25 percent (the United States, in
terms of GNP) is doing the opposite. We can mobilise by example, by
the way we live, by being part of a shift in values towards more
sustainable lifestyles – but we cannot wait for this to happen.
Governments have to set the framework; NGOs and the media have
to lead opinion.

We can also mobilise through international co-operation. We need to
start with Europe to build a vision of security there, to create the professional, functioning instruments for human security, markets and environmental protection that others will copy and join. Then we need to
widen the consensus – build on the changes taking place in American
public opinion; create a coalition with India, China and others – so that
all understand that development, security and a sustainable environment are all a part of the same shared problem. And that the problem
can only be solved together.

4 | The British in partnership with the developing world

Vandana Shiva

Britain was the leader of the colonial empire. No country has its history – and its future – more intimately connected to people in remote regions throughout the world, especially in Africa and Asia. History has placed British citizens firmly within the web of global relationships. The opportunity now exists to turn these relationships into the foundations of a real global citizenship and global democracy.

Between now and 2025, British citizens have a choice between being consumers in a global supermarket – inhabitants in a fortress of privilege – or becoming members of the global family.

The trajectory of Britain's development is intimately linked to that of the South. If Britain strengthens its solidarity with communities in developing countries, a new shared vision of global democracy can emerge, in which every citizen is of equal value, and their right to their share of the ecological space on the planet is respected.

It is not only Britain that is at a crossroads. The developing world is too. Either we will move towards further non-sustainability and social and economic polarisation or we will move together towards sustainability, social harmony and peace and economic justice.

Energy, water and food will be three areas where these choices will be most dramatic. The energy future of Britain, and relatedly of the South, will be based either on more greenhouse gas emissions (and therefore more climate instability) with a new rush towards nuclear energy, or the South and developed countries like Britain will move towards renewable energy sources like solar and wind power.

Similarly, Britain will either push for the privatization and commodification of water through GATS (the General Agreement of Trade and Services in the World Trade Organisation) or Britain will join the movement for water democracy, which sees water as a public good and a common resource. Britain will either submit to the WTO ruling on genetically modified crops, or lead the way to a GMO-free world and the establishment of food democracy.

British citizens should not see intervention in developing countries as an option to choose – it is already happening every day. A recent article in *The Independent* showed that a 50 gram bag of salad costs 99p but wastes almost 50 litres of water. A mixed salad takes 300 litres.[1] As Bruce Laneford of the University of East Anglia has said, "we are exporting drought". Global retail chains like Tesco, Sainsbury's and Walmart are increasingly sourcing fruit and vegetables from Africa and India. This is leading to large scale uprooting and destitution of farmers, and is contributing to drought and desertification, while increasing 'food miles' and undermining food security and food sovereignty. While India is being made to grow vegetables for Europe, we are also being forced to import pesticide-laden wheat in spite of massive domestic wheat production, further threatening farmers' livelihoods.

India has suffered 21 droughts since the beginning of the last century. In all, 1,391,841,000 people were affected and of them 4,250,430 died. Such disasters are likely to increase with climate change.

The agriculture of the South is biodiverse, prudent with its use of water and very drought resilient. And it is being destroyed precisely when diverse and decentralised systems need to be conserved to reduce the impact of climate change and increase our resilience to it. On the one hand, drought is increasing as a result of climate change. On the other hand it is increasing due to globalisation of the food supply and the diversion of the land and water of food communities of the South to produce cheap food for the North.

The poor are thus paying three times over – through increased vulnerability to climate change, through increased water scarcity, and through the uprooting of communities from their land, villages and homes to make way for wasteful globalised trade. Cyclones and sea level rises are other aspects of climate disasters. A one metre rise in sea level is projected to displace 7.1 million people and submerge about 5,764 sq km of land along with 4,200 km of roads in India. The economic loss for Mumbai alone would be 23 to 30 billion Rupees. A glimpse of climate disaster was experienced in June 2005 in Mumbai when 900 mm rain came down in one day, flooding the city and bringing life to a total halt.

Over the past 20 years, I have built Navdanya, India's biodiversity and organic farming movement. We are increasingly realising there is a convergence between the objectives of conserving biodiversity, reducing the impact of climate change and alleviating poverty. Biodiverse, local, organic systems produce more food and higher farm incomes while also reducing water use and the risk of crop failure due to climate change. Increasing the biodiversity of farming systems can reduce contribution to drought. Millets, which are far more nutritious than rice and wheat, use only 200-300 mm water, compared to 2500 mm needed for Green Revolution rice farming. India could grow four times more food using millets. However, global trade is pushing agriculture to GMO monocultures of corn, soya, canola and cotton, worsening vulnerability to climate change.

Biodiversity offers us the resilience to recover from climate disasters. After the super-cyclone in 1999 killed 10,000 people in Orissa on the east coast of India, and after the tsunami in 2004, Navdanya distributed seeds of saline-resistant varieties of rice to rejuvenate agriculture in lands made saline by the sea. We called them 'Seeds of Hope'. We are now creating seed banks of drought-resistant, flood-resistant and saline-resistant seed varieties to respond to the extremes brought about by climate change.

Climate chaos creates uncertainty. Diversity offers a cushion against both climate extremes and climate uncertainty. Diversity and decentralisation are the dual principles in building economies that are not reliant on oil and in dealing with the climate vulnerability that is the residue of the age of oil.

This will require also some fundamental change. Within the European concept of property, for example, capital is the only kind of investment with value. Therefore it treats returns on capital investment as the only kind that needs protection. Many non-Western indigenous communities and cultures recognise that investments can also be of labour or of care and nurturance. Such cultural systems protect investments beyond capital. They protect the culture of conservation and the culture of caring and sharing. They recognise that vital resources like water and biodiversity are a shared common good, not a commodity or private property. The enclosures of the commons, which started in Britain in the nineteenth century, continue today under the label of globalisation.

The land, the water, the biodiversity, the labour of people in the south are literally being consumed by the European model of development, leaving devastated ecosystems, and displaced and impoverished communities. A sustainable Britain has to stop this predation of the planet.

The poor are paying three times over – through climate change, water scarcity, and the uprooting of communities from their land, villages and homes.

This change towards sustainability would simultaneously be a change in the mind and a change in lifestyle. It would be a paradigm shift; a shift in production and consumption patterns that would give everyone their rightful share to the Earth's resources.

Governments cannot create such changes. People must lead. This means people on the ground changing society and the economy to help create justice and sustainability through their everyday actions, in their homes and in the market, in schools and in the workplace. Then the British people of 2025 will truly be members of the global family.

References

1   'The real cost of a bag of salad: You pay 99p, Africa pays 50 litres of fresh water', Jeremy Laurance, *The Independent*, 29 April 2006

5 | Learning lessons from the future

Michelle Harrison

Twenty years on

Between Live Aid and Live 8 the lives of British people changed quite a lot. On the whole, we got richer and busier. The leisure economy grew exponentially and, with it, international travel. Experiences became as valued as material things. The summer calendar of festivals extended year on year, as did the age of those who considered themselves young enough to attend. Single issue politics and 'ethical' consumption went mainstream as party politics became a minority interest. Growing economic inequalities encouraged social fragmentation. Affluent consumers began to reshape the nature of their relationships with businesses through increasing expectations of transparency and responsibility. Astounding changes in connectivity utterly transformed the way in which we communicated locally and globally.

By 2005 the original lyrics of Band Aid's 1984 single 'Feed the World' seemed worse than naff. Over the previous 20 years the academic discourse that had reshaped the perspective of the North on the South had filtered out into the public consciousness. Issues of social and environmental justice were understood to be firmly linked. Despite – or perhaps because of – an increasingly visual culture, we were no less appalled by images of stricken humanity. Twenty years on, we were even more willing to get on the phone or the street to participate in development 'events'.

Between 1985 and 2005 the wider world changed a great deal and yet had changed hardly at all. Global inequalities seem just as intractable. British people remain confused about who is responsible and who is accountable for international social justice, and in particular, around the role that they as individuals play. Contemporary consumers are almost all in some way or other 'modal' – their individual actions being determined over the course of a day, a week or a year by the specific circumstances of the moment. Only a tiny proportion of people are consistently 'ethical' or 'environmental' in their consumption patterns. Not everyone who marched on Gleneagles to challenge the government to address global inequities bothered to vote in the national elections. Plenty of those wearing white wristbands demonstrating allegiance to fair trade also wear clothing made in sweatshops. Climate change campaigners and activists fly around the world from conference to conference. Many of us demand action of others yet reinforce the linkages of inequality by our own everyday consumption choices.

We were like this as a nation in 1985 and we are like it even more now, by virtue of the fact that our growing affluence has opened up for us more opportunities to choose and to consume. British consumers, like affluent consumers across the North, are living lives ridden by countless apparent contradictions. Added up together, they are encouraging a curious type of status quo within our own societies and within the global conundrum of trade, aid and politics.

In another 20 years, what degree of change are we likely to see? Will there be a fundamental paradigm shift or not? How will British attitudes towards global social and environmental problems evolve between now and 2025? Who will be held responsible for solving these problems? How will British people view the role of government, corporations, NGOs and themselves, in terms of responsibility and accountability? How will individual behaviour patterns shift, and how will this influence global geopolitical structures?

Gleneagles and Live 8, like Live Aid before them, represented a latent energy and drive for a global social justice. The challenge for stakeholders – and it is not insubstantial – is for this energy to be nurtured and grown and transformed into everyday actions and triumphs. As with all strategic thinking, in order to do this both the present circumstances and the drivers that will shape outcomes in the future need to be understood. The logical, plausible extremities to which the next 20 years could take us need to be explored and the outcomes that can and cannot be influenced need to be considered. Most importantly, the opportunities and the threats – the drivers of continual stasis or the dissipation of interest – need to be assessed. We need to learn from the future.

Learning from the future

Scenarios of the future are not predictions. They are coherent and plausible views of possible futures. The future can not be predicted unless all the variables are known and of course, they never can be. Futures work is about rehearsal: the drivers of change have the potential to create multiple possible futures and through building scenarios, the 'universe' of future outcomes can be considered. The future is likely to include elements of all the scenarios that such an exercise creates. It is certain to be messy, diverse and complex.

A scenario development process enables organisations and stakeholders to take some responsibility for their future. Scenarios generate a strategic conversation about how to prepare for uncertainty and they provide a way for organisations and individuals to start to think seriously and practically about what could lie ahead.[1] They help diverse stakeholders understand each other's values and desires for future outcomes. They bring to the surface the opportunities and threats that future strategy needs to harness or mitigate.[2]

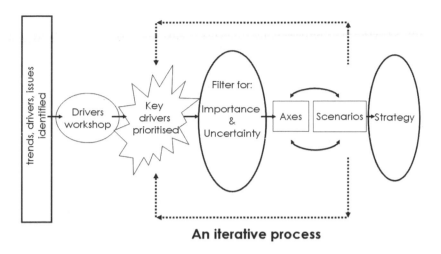

An iterative process

Figure 1 Scenario planning: a typical process   *Source: HCHLV*

Our aim here is to use a scenario planning process to explore how British attitudes towards global social and environmental justice will evolve between now and 2025, and, in line with this, to whom responsibility and accountability for action will be accorded. Figure 1 outlines the process which – in the simplest of terms – involves the generation of an exhaustive list of all of the trends and drivers that could potentially influence the outcome (the evolution of British attitudes), followed by a process of prioritisation of drivers which filter this number down until the most significant remain. These key drivers are then analysed to determine how important (dominant) and uncertain they are. The drivers considered most important, yet most uncertain, create the 'axes of uncertainty' around which the scenarios are built.

Most importantly, any views of the future, whether built around scenarios, trends or statistical models, are only as good as the analysis of current circumstances – the basis upon which the future is built. Key here are the societal characteristics that shape our attitudes to global social and environmental justice and influence our ability to 'act out'

29

our beliefs. Some of these are both far more mundane – and far more profound – than many campaigners or politicians may wish to believe.

The current landscape

Between Live Aid and Live 8 the British population saw their real disposable income double.[3] Indeed, since 2000, disposable income has increased by 20 percent. This growth has fuelled the expansion of the 'experience' economy; over the 1990s the rate of growth of consumer expenditure in leisure services was more than double that of the average growth rates of all goods. It also shifted consumer expectations in a fundamental way. In the course of a single decade, our presumptions about our entitlements to eat, drink and be merry, to take minibreaks and holidays, and to achieve self-actualisation through new, ever more exciting experiences, exploded. This new environment of 'entitlement' makes the social and environmental trade-offs from our actions harder to reconcile: we understand, for instance, the impact of our overseas mini-breaks or long-haul holidays but we are also aware, as one inter-viewee commented recently, that 'the plane is leaving the runway whether I'm on it or not'.

The 'experience economy' has filtered through the whole of society but is enjoyed mostly by the 'mass affluent'. It's often noted that income growth has been at the expense of equality. It's old news too that our material and experiential wealth is not making us happier: at the end of the 1990s, only 45 percent of British people agreed that they were happy with their standard of living as compared to 58 percent a decade earlier.

Affluence has had an interesting effect on the value that people place on their individual resources. At the time of Live Aid, the consumer currency of exchange was money. By the time of Live 8, it was time and energy. In crude terms, the 1980s were about money and getting more of it while the 1990s were about coping with the lack of time that resulted from our revved-up lives. Since the beginning of the new decade, the focus has been on energy and this is a fast-moving trend. Last year more than half the population felt too low in energy by the evening to do anything other than sit down. This has driven our national obsession with personal wellbeing. It also helps us understand the apparent lack of connection between people's beliefs and actions, or their 'modality' (why the behaviours or values are swayed by the specific circumstances of the moment). We wish to live well but often lack the time or energy to recycle, reconnect, campaign or even shop for more ethical products. We also find it hard to relinquish our 'right' to have a personally interesting or fulfiling experience, be it focused on travel, the interiors of our homes, or shopping.

There is no evidence to suggest that between Live Aid and Live 8 British people became less concerned about international social and environmental justice. But there is strong evidence that during this period a shift occurred in the perceptions of need and entitlement within our society. Over the course of the 1990s we saw a steady decline in a belief in the entitlement of the poorest in Britain to receive help from the state, and an increase in the perception that British people in poverty are responsible for their own circumstances. As many social campaigners have already realised, the perceived 'worthiness' of those at the bottom of our own society has declined. A greater understanding of the debt and trade trap seems to have accorded an increased 'worthiness' to the international dispossessed. In parallel, within our own affluent society, the poorest are viewed less as the victims of structural inequities and more as the victims of the inevitable conditions of modern life.

Alongside this has been a steady growth in a simplistic individualism. For the last 20 years Henley have been asking people on an annual basis whether they believe that the quality of life in Britain is best improved by looking after the community's interests 'rather than simply their own'; or looking after themselves 'which ultimately raises the standards for everyone'. For the first time in a decade we have recorded a majority of people suggesting that looking after themselves first is the best way to improve the quality of life in Britain. A change is in the air, and it is being led by people of lower socio-economic groups. People in social groups C2DE are currently more likely to opt for the individualistic stance than their more affluent fellow citizens.

This apparent rise in individualism does, however, have some interesting and complex manifestations. A much more significant proportion of British people, for instance, accept their own personal role and responsibility for climate change – both for being at fault for causing it and for responsibility for tackling it – than many of their counterparts from other parts of the North.[4] Strikingly, they perceive individuals – consumers – to be more 'at fault' for causing climate change than service sector industries, and more 'responsible for tackling it' than any corporate sectors. (Greater responsibility for tackling damage to the environment and climate change is accorded more to government and NGOs than it is to the service sector.) The data suggests a perspective of shared responsibility between stakeholders. Without doubt, this recognition of the complexity of the problem is a further driver of 'contradictory' behaviour on the part of consumers.

The key drivers of change

So, within the current consumer landscape we have some strong clues about the nature of the opportunities and constraints for energising the British to engage in a sustained campaign for international social and environmental justice. Our key question now is: how might this landscape shift over the next twenty years? What are the key drivers and forces for change for British attitudes toward global social and environmental problems to 2025?

A team from Henley Centre Headlight Vision applied a scenario planning process to this question. To begin, a 'drivers pack' was generated, with more than 60 potential trends and issues that could potentially influence change. We then went through the stages outlined in

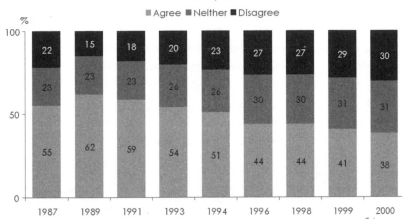

Figure 2 Fewer people feel that the government should spend money on the poor *per se*

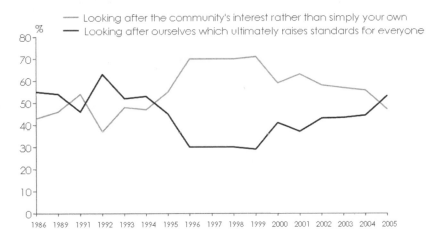

Figure 3 It's all about me or all about us?

Thinking of damage to the environment and climate change, who do you think is at fault for causing it?

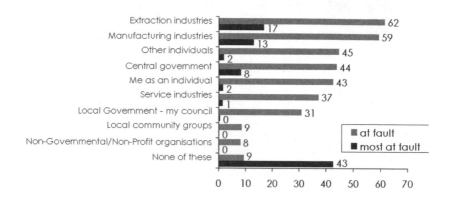

Thinking of damage to the environment and climate change, who do you think is responsible for tackling it?

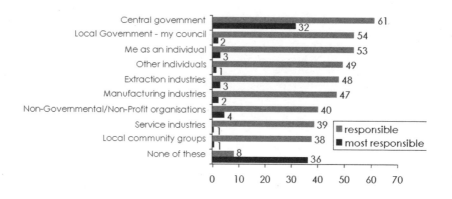

Figure 4 Who is at fault and who is responsible?

60 drivers of change

Ageing population
Changing household set-up
Rise of personal mobility
Increased migration
Globalisation
Urbanisation of culture
Growing importance of developing economies
Changing structure of the UK economy
Continued rise of the 'experience economy'
Convenience-driven consumers
'Always on' society
Information overload
Increasing capability of electronic networks
Embedded technology
Developing environmental technologies
Increasing consumer environmental awareness
Perceptions of climate change
Risk of energy shortfall
Increasing water scarcity
Changing rural land use
Depletion of biotic resources
Increased focus on waste
Long term UK economic stability
Increasing social inequality
Deepening consumption culture
Shifting community values
Increased focus on wellbeing
Rise of the empowered consumer
Rise of single issue politics
Rise in extremism
Increasing pressure on public spending
The new localism
Continued rise of big business
Declining trust in institutions

Risk averse society
Continued rise of China
Continued rise of India
Uncertain future of international governance
Changing attitudes towards US
Future of Europe
Changing nature of environmental legislation
Role of self-interest in responding to environmental pressure
Shifting sense of responsibility
Rise of new networks
A rise in black and grey market
Material to mental
Time and energy deficit
Spend now, save later
Move towards hypothecation
Rise of offshoring
Increasing carbon awareness
'Corruption' in developing countries
Increasing foreign investment
Growing political and economic importance of developing countries
Growing NGO activity
Growing access to media in developing countries
Continuing gender inequality
Growing access to credit
Supply chain technologies
Increasing fragmentation of media
Increasing focus on value
Ethical consumption growing globally
Changing corporate roles
Retuned to nature
Authenticity

Figure 5 Drivers of change

Figure 1, assessing and prioritising drivers, until those felt to be of most importance were identified. These were then each considered, in terms of their degree of relative dominance and uncertainty. From this, the set of axes for the generation of the scenarios, together with the components of the scenarios themselves, were developed.

Identifying the key drivers provides a partial story of possible change. In reality, the drivers will manifest themselves in multiple ways across different social groups. They will also interact, collide with and contradict one another. Indeed, it is critical to understand the very real contradictory nature of many of the overlapping trends and drivers. Within this framework we can consider the drivers that have the greatest capability or likelihood of dominating and shaping the landscape, and ultimately, the environment within which British people will think through and act out their beliefs.

The trends and issues that were considered ranged across the political, economic, social, technological and environmental spheres. The potential for rising energy costs contrasted with developing environmental technologies. The growing role of the third sector was as significant as the potential for the mainstreaming of green issues in the political sphere. Modal consumption culture, the time and energy deficit and the experience economy presented key tensions, in relation to acting upon our perceptions of climate change and increased focus on health and wellbeing. Meanwhile, the medium term stability of the UK economy is fundamental to the ability and willingness of consumers to respond to any needs beyond their own.

Under the technological drivers, the rise of global connectivity contrasted with the trend towards information overload, where consumers are quite literally collapsing into stasis under the overwhelming number of contradictory messages in the media. At the same time, affluent food cultures and new technologies are driving the increasing importance of provenance.

Our changing household set up (and in particular, the growth in single person households) has the potential to lead to more wasteful consumption, given the lack of economies of scale. The rise of the child free (the government predicts that one in four women born in 1972 will not have children) has the potential to reinforce this trend.

Within the realm of business trends, the growth of the 'hourglass economy' is important. Business models for most retailers are continuing to focus on value. At the same time we are seeing a significant growth in high-end retailing. Discounters and own brand labels are both on the rise, as are specialist high-end markets for consumers keen to buy into a sense of affluence, sophistication and indulgence. More widely, the rising demand for corporations to play a wider role than simply maximising investor returns means that changing corporate roles will continue to shift the balance in responsibility between government and business.

There are multiple geo-political drivers of change that will shape British attitudes towards overseas need and entitlement. The perception of a rise in extremism on a global level is not just a trend but a significant potential wildcard: a sustained series of terrorist attacks in the UK, for instance, would almost certainly derail other trends. The changing nature of US influence over the next 20 years and the rise of China and India will influence some of the international dimensions of responsibility for global social and environmental justice. Closer to home, the new localism and shifting community values capture changing personal networks and geographical focus. Both trends are currently manifesting themselves variously across different socio-economic groups.

Scenarios of the future

Scenarios are not forecasts or predictions. Through building scenarios, the 'universe' of future outcomes can be considered, allowing stakeholders to understand each other's values and desires for future outcomes, and think seriously and practically about what could lie

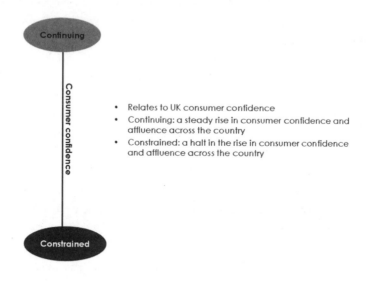

Figure 6 The vertical axis

- Relates to the means by which people achieve quality of life
- 'Focus on individual': here, the prevailing consumer attitude is one that focuses on self rather than the wider community. UK consumers seek to achieve quality of life by pursuing personal experiences and decreasing their own time and energy deficit
- Focus on community: quality of life is sought out through engagement with the wider community, whether it be local, national or international.

Figure 7 The horizontal axis

ahead. The future is likely to include elements of all the scenarios that a planning exercise generates. Our goal is to consider what scenario planners refer to as the 'edge' of plausible futures. At some point in time, future outcomes may also shift substantially as a result of a 'wild-card' or a sudden intensification of a trend. A series of 'shocking' mani-festations of climate change during the next five to ten years, for instance, would have a fundamental impact on British attitudes to global environmental issues. (Obviously, under a formal scenario plan-ning process, such wildcards or 'shocks' are identified within the strategy as key triggers for re-evaluation.)

Through a process of filtering and clustering, the 60 or so trends listed in Figure 5 were prioritised. What emerged were two clear areas of dominant, yet uncertain activity, which form the central set of axes for the scenarios.

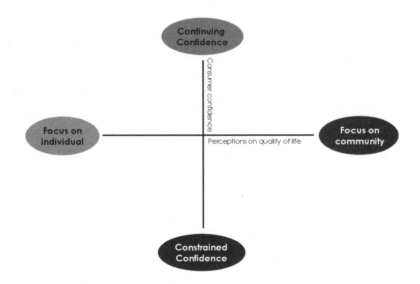

Figure 8 Defining the axes

The horizontal axis is about perceptions of quality of life: this relates to the means by which British people will believe that they achieve their quality of life. 'Focus on individual', where the prevailing consumer attitude is one that focuses on the self rather than the wider community contrasts with 'focus on community', where the quality of life is sought out through engagement with the wider community, be it local, national or international.

The vertical axis is concerned with UK consumer confidence: this relates not just to relative affluence but to the perceptions that consumers have of the economy, how it will perform into the future and how it will affect their household. Under conditions of high confidence, there is a continuing rise in affluence across the country and a belief that the economy will remain strong. Under conditions of low confidence, relative affluence is either declining or consumers are expecting it to.

These axes generate the boundary space within which the four contrasting scenarios of 2025 are drawn – depicting the environment within which British attitudes towards global social and environmental problems are determined and the roles accorded to government, companies and NGOs.

Perhaps the surprising element of the scenarios depicted in Figure 9 is their insularity. The scenario planning process that was undertaken by the Henley team generated over 60 drivers including multiple trends with global dimensions. Through the prioritisation process, however, the trends that came through were, on balance, trends acted out on the British rather than international stage. The dynamics of the household and the individual, the desire for experience, the management of time and energy, and a focus on health and well being are balanced against – and even have the potential to cancel out – issues of national politics and international social and environmental concerns.

Our goal, then, is to consider the 'edge' of plausible futures. Therefore the scenarios that follow read to some extent as caricatures. For the purposes of this article, the titles too have an element of caricature. The purpose is not to choose between 'good' or 'bad' or 'likely' or 'unlikely' scenarios but to consider the strategic implications for each group of stakeholders under different future conditions.

References

1   See 'Scenarios: The Art of Strategic Conversation', Kees van der Hiejden, John Wiley and Sons, 1996.

2   For those who would like to read more, Lawrence Wilkinson's *How to build scenarios* offers a good start. See www.wired.com/wired/scenarios/build.html.

3   Unless otherwise stated, all data is derived from Henley Centre Headlight Vision's 'Planning for Consumer Change' proprietary social research programme.

4   This comes from 'HenleyWorld', the proprietary global tracking survey of Henley Centre Headlight Vision. At the time of going to press, the initial analysis of 'HenleyWorld' 2006 is being undertaken.

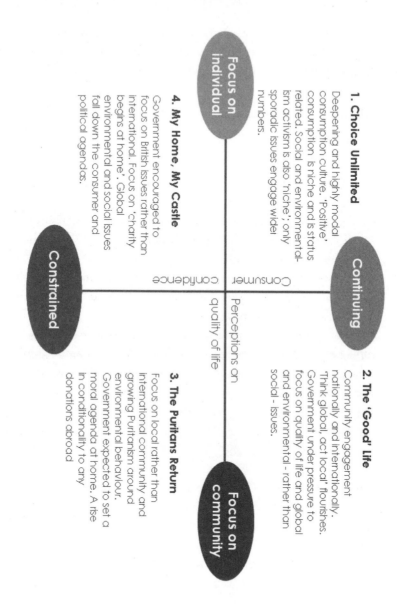

Figure 9 The scenarios

1. Choice Unlimited

Deepening and highly modal consumption culture. 'Positive' consumption is niche and is status related. Social and environmental-ism activism is also 'niche'; only sporadic issues engage wider numbers.

2. The 'Good' Life

Community engagement nationally and internationally. 'Think global, act local' flourishes. Government under pressure to focus on quality of life and global and environmental - rather than social - issues.

3. The Puritans Return

Focus on local rather than international community and growing Puritanism around environmental behaviour. Government expected to set a moral agenda at home. A rise in conditionality to any donations abroad

4. My Home, My Castle

Government encouraged to focus on British issues rather than international. Focus on 'charity begins at home'. Global environmental and social issues fall down the consumer and political agendas.

Focus on individual

Focus on community

Constrained

Continuing

Consumer confidence

Perceptions on quality of life

The British in 2025: four scenarios

Scenario one:

Choice Unlimited

In this scenario, there has been a continual growth of consumer spending. The retail and leisure sectors are blurred and interchangeable. The nation (and early evening television) is hugely interested in storage. Storage companies have continued to be a major growth sector and have diversified beyond furniture: these days people rent space to store their clothes, domestic appliances and even their china. Personal home stylists are as common as 'actualisation' coaches – everyone has one – and are employed to interchange and 'refresh' wardrobes, kitchen and interiors on a monthly or six-weekly basis. Despite the continuing socio-economic inequalities, even the poorest in society can afford to shop more than they used to.

Under this scenario, in 2025 nearly half the population are living in single person households. Waste, congestion levels and international travel have continued to grow. (Last year package holidays to the Antarctic outstripped those to the Caribbean for the first time.)

'Positive' and 'ethical' consumption has grown in line with the growth of the economy as a whole. Some of the 'fair trade' brands have become status symbols, relating to the provenance of high-end coffees and chocolate. However, the most significant growth area in the food sector has been nutraceuticals, as the focus on well-being has led to the development of more and more personalised 'medically enhanced' food products.

Social and environmental activism is a strong 'niche' area of the leisure economy. Under this scenario, Oxfam and Greenpeace compete to be known for giving the best parties and, in order to maintain crowd numbers at campaigning rallies, now market them as festivals. Their aid, debt and trade and environmental campaigns get less web site hits than the online dating agencies that they sponsor. Voluntary Services Overseas has no problems attracting volunteers – in fact, VSO holidays are very popular with single thirty-somethings – but 'experience minibreaks' have replaced the longer sojourn in popularity. Global inequalities continue to grow and thus have created new opportunities for 'extreme' holidays in the slum districts in the cities of developing countries.

Under this scenario, national government is continuing to focus on economic growth and less than ten percent of people vote in the local authority elections. Trade and aid issues remain on the political agenda thanks to continued NGO lobbying. But consumer pressure is weak – even single issue campaigns are failing to achieve genuine political momentum.

In recent years some of the biggest corporations have managed to down-size or close their CSR departments. There has been very little consumer outcry. The marketing focus is increasingly personalised and has shifted towards one-to-one strategies.

Scenario two:

The 'Good' Life

In this scenario, growing consumer affluence and confidence has encouraged a greater shift towards a community-focused approach to quality of life. Community engagement has grown, even in relatively poorer neighbourhoods, and 'think global, act local' flourishes. While people's working lives continue as before with executives still averaging 50 hour weeks, there has been a cultural shift towards 'slower' family time. Leisure time has become more focused on the quality of home life and the neighbourhood environment. Business travel has continued unabated but international leisure travel has actually flattened out as people seek to be re-energised through their local networks of friends and family. Car-free family holidays are now the norm, even though they are mostly enjoyed overseas. Both the executive from the City and the creative director from advertising devote Saturday mornings to maintaining their microgenerators and allotments. Green issues are so mainstream in national politics that the Green Party is now consigned to the history books.

Many neighbourhoods – even those urban villages with a significant socio-economic mix – have 'mend and share' schemes, and once a month the local church or school commonly host a 'barter day'. Recently the multiple retailers have been offering warehouse space for community storage as part of their 'life partners' framework. As 'community twinning' has replaced 'town twinning', some retailers are even paying for the transport of unneeded household items to be sent overseas to the 'foster community' in the South. Fair trade is now an entry level requirement for food and clothing retailers but the focus on locally-produced products is central. These days, it would be a social *faux pas* of the worst kind to cater for a dinner party with produce grown overseas.

There has been a significant increase both in multi-generational family living and in multi-person occupancy. 'Granny flats' are automatically built on new homes designed for families. Meanwhile, the increasing numbers of single and child-free people are more often living in multi-let premises with adult 'common rooms'.

The majority of households now have direct debits set up to charities. These days however, those who donate to international development charities make a direct debit into the bank account of the female head of household of the family that they sponsor. Under this scenario the NGOs compete for the role of 'best international connector'. They also have developed a strong brand around long haul travel advice: helping travellers do 'the maximum overland and the minimum over cloud', and connecting them to 'host' communities and households where, for a donation, they can experience a 'deepening' cultural interchange. Interest in debt, trade and aid issues remains strong but it is climate change that has risen to the top of the political agenda. Citizens are actively concerned about the threat to their quality of life posed by climate change and national governments are struggling to force through compliance issues in Asia.

Government is expected to consider local 'quality of life' issues in all areas of public policy. Continuing problems with the national public transport system are regular front page news and the Minister for Quality of Life is under pressure. Under this scenario, some constituencies have higher rates of turnout in local authority elections than in national general elections.

Corporations have expanded their CSR portfolios to include their 'glocal' work, and how they focus on community level action across the planet. Supermarket store managers are now trained in community engagement techniques. At the headquarters of many multinational retailers, the new CSR role for 'glocal linkages' are being created, where electronic vouchers collected in British communities can be traded in by the 'twinned community' in selected sub-Saharan countries for food and goods. Under consumer pressure, multiple commodity chains have been reformulated and local store managers are incentivised to reduce ever lower the collective food miles purchased by their customers.

Scenario three:

The Puritans Return

Under conditions of low consumer confidence, people have increasingly focused on their local needs rather than their international linkages. Under this scenario there has been a growth of 'puritanism' around lifestyle issues. But it is complex: there are significant cultural differences between different social groups. Whilst the 'moral' majority lament the throwaway culture of others, the liberal minorities lament the growing cultural strength of the new puritans.

There are further cultural divides opening up between families and the child-free, now a quarter of the adult population. Under this scenario, working parents and those staying at home by choice are debating the new cultural issues: are working parents who employ a steady stream of household 'helpers' to manage their time and energy actually engaging in unnecessary and excessive consumption?

Under this scenario, the poorest are now viewed by the 'masses' as 'undeserving'. The socio-economic and cultural split is reinforced through the retail and leisure sectors. In affluent neighbourhoods local independently owned retailing has developed a moral overtone. In poorer neighbourhoods, a variety of low-cost British, American and European chains dominate and the takeaway food culture remains very strong.

Under this scenario, aid, debt and trade issues are on the domestic agenda at key times in the international political calendar. The liberal middle classes are supportive of these issues but amongst the moral majority it is acceptable to talk about the cultural aspects of global inequalities. Some newspaper columnists used strong moralistic over-tones in their discussion of the political economy of some African states. Environmental issues are strongly politicised: government is under pressure to sever trade ties with the Asian and sub-Saharan economies still failing to take action against climate change.

The international development NGOs are, under this scenario, increasingly focusing on domestic poverty and inequality, in an attempt to encourage a greater degree of compassion for the most needy in British society. There is significant concern for the levels of personal indebtedness amongst poorer people – which are rising steeply after a period of stability. The national focus is also driven by the desire of some of the development NGOs to disassociate themselves from the hostility and conflict that the international social and environmental agendas are now attracting. Those with a 'liberal' branding are finding themselves increasingly attacked by those who want to see a 'hard line' approach to the Southern states that are failing to conform to climate control standards.

Under this scenario, international travel has declined amongst the more affluent who are concerned about redundancy and their pensions, as well as the environment. Cut price international minibreaks have overtaken the longer package holidays amongst the lower middle classes.

Amongst the moral majority however, lift-sharing schemes flourish as oil prices rise and the recycling of clothing and household durables is now undertaken in more affluent neighbourhoods. Families link up at the neighbourhood level with people 'like them' to pass clothes down to younger children or share ownership of cars. More and more people walk or cycle to work to maintain their well-being and fitness.

Government is under pressure to set a moral agenda at home while at the same time controlling inflation. There is strong pressure to reduce aid donations unless attached to stringent conditions. National election turnouts are higher than they have ever been – in this climate politics have never been more divided and is once again fashionable.

Corporations are under pressure from the city and their shareholders, and in multiple, different ways, from their customers. Never has marketing been so complex. On the one hand the push for continuing deep value is putting pressure on their margins, and, on the other, their CSR policies are attracting hostile attention from different campaigning groups, each with different demands.

Scenario four:

My Home, My Castle

Under this scenario, conditions of low stability are encouraging individualistic 'retreat'. Community suspicion and the rise of the 'my home is my castle' mentality has grown. Even the liberal middle classes are persuaded these days that charity begins at home; the weaker economic climate is leading to pressure on the affluent as well as the poorest, and concerns about international development issues and climate change fell below the radar once house prices started to fall. Global environmental and social issues are low down both the consumer and political agendas: the focus is on employment, access to healthcare and pensions.

Under this scenario, deep value discounters flourish in food and clothing retail. The ethical food sector is withering. The focus is on 'pure value': slick delivery models that focus on bottom line value rather than social equity. Retail commodity chains have become ever slicker, sourcing globally for the lowest prices and moving on quickly when necessary. The 'domestic professional' sector is also shrinking. With falling employment and low consumer confidence, even the middle classes are cutting back on their time-saving employees. Well-being and lifestyle magazines are struggling in a shrinking marketplace.

Personal transport costs have escalated, as have the costs of basic household bills. People are looking to save money on food and clothing. International travel is less common, but only because the lower middle classes are so worried about their falling equity. Gated communities and CCTV cameras have proliferated in a climate of distrust.

NGOs associated with international causes have seen falling membership. Indeed, across the third sector there has been a slump in participation and membership. In order to survive, charities are associating themselves with national issues and especially those around the care needs of the elderly who are increasingly viewed as the new 'dispossessed'.

Government is under pressure to cut taxes but also needs to invest in public services. This is a difficult time to make redistributive tax measures however. While middle class people are seeing their pension funds shrink there is little room for domestic manoeuvres. International development is now low on the agenda. With oil prices so high, the government is focusing on the economy and the City. Right now, it is hard for politicians to focus on the longer-term commitment needed to shift to a different model of energy generation and use.

Under this scenario, CSR reporting has shifted towards the employee rather than the supplier. Companies are under acute pressure to dramatically extend private health and education provision for employees as well as re-instate pension benefits. One corporate supermarket chain has recently gone as far as to open its own schools for its employees' children. Left-of-centre social commentators bemoan the role that corporations are playing in driving forward the growing 'social apartheid' in Britain.

The questions raised: who will we be?

Each of the scenarios depicts potential manifestations of trends that are already with us in some way or other in British society. Choice Unlimited has a bit of an air of 'business as usual' about it. In some ways The 'Good' Life feels not too dissimilar to the current weekend atmosphere of some of London's most affluent urban villages. The Puritans Return and My Home, My Castle perhaps seem a little more extreme. But, in 2006, we are looking at this scenario from the perspective of a society that has enjoyed many years of sustained economic growth. Those of us who remember the collapse of house prices fifteen years ago may feel more familiar with the territory.

These scenarios are rehearsals. We know that the future could dish up any mix of these potential extremes. The scenarios are not laden with value judgements themselves, but they certainly should invite them. If we want to catalyse change, they also invite questions about what our responsibilities and different roles should be.

- **Who will decide?**
  Just how much power or influence do different stakeholders have in driving, shaping and responding to the most dominant and uncertain trends? Certainly, the main drivers of quality of life and consumer confidence are beyond the ultimate control of any single stakeholder group, but government has a strong role to play. There is room here too for value-driven leadership from the NGO community but they have to be clear what it is they are driving for. A fundamental paradigm shift in behaviours amongst more affluent groups could come at the expense of social cohesion in Britain. We need to be careful what we ask for.

- **Who leads?**
  How much leadership are corporations willing to exercise? Which corporations – in which sectors – are required to take the

lead? Under conditions of economic constraint, would the current generation of CEOs drop CSR like a hot potato? Have we yet seen a shift fundamental enough to be sustained through times of tightening profit margins? Or has CSR so far been just a useful marketing tool?

■ **What are the lessons for campaigners?**
Which trends would NGOs and campaigners wish to see intensify? What societal values do citizens wish to see dominating the landscape? Would NGOs be willing to go along with prevailing cultural trends in order to sustain membership and popularity? How far would they go?

■ **What are the lessons for government?**
The scenarios – particularly Choice Unlimited – raise the question of how far government and other policy makers should go to encourage people to translate their beliefs into actions. What can government do to make it as easy as possible to engage? In particular, what does it mean for DFID, who, under different conditions, could see their longer terms strategies become more or less aligned to the changing political consensus? What are the implications for the public policy of citizenship, nationally and globally?

The scenarios remind us of the vulnerability of social ideals. They remind us of the speed at which we can shift our priorities as consumers and the short-term perspective within which we understand or imagine our own security. Under conditions of consumer confidence, we will spend money but we are less generous with our time.

Under conditions of a lack of consumer confidence, the tendency will be towards less generosity with both. The challenge for all stakeholders is to shake up the consumer myopia. To persistently communicate the wider perspective and explain the linkages that bind people globally, in mutual dependence, as citizens. These are not insignificant challenges. But the size of the prize is huge.